"The purpose of this book is to glorify the Lord and not any one person."

—JOAN BEVERLY WEBEL JOHNSON
OCTOBER 11, 1980

Though this book is written in memory of my dear wife, Joan Beverly Webel Johnson, she had a hand in its creation. A notebook and pencil were always available beside our bed in which to write specific statements or revelations, word for word. Her writings were the inspiration for this book. Her quotes, along with the dates and times they were written, can be found throughout the pages that follow.

The reader and "Bill have to believe completely that Jesus is speaking through Joan."

To protect the people in our story, full names are not used, except for the names of Reverend Oral Roberts, Joan, and me.

—F. WILLIAM JOHNSON

This is Joan's story . . .

The

Little One

Her Life,
Visit to Heaven, &
Messages from the Lord

F. WILLIAM JOHNSON

HIGHERLIFE
DEVELOPMENT SERVICES, INC.
Oviedo, Florida

The Little One: Her Life, Visit to Heaven, & Messages from the Lord

by F. William Johnson
Published by HigherLife Development Services, Inc.
400 Fontana Circle
Building 1 – Suite 105
Oviedo, Florida 32765
(407) 563-4806
www.ahigherlife.com

Unless otherwise identified, scripture quotations are from the *The Holy Bible: King James Version*. Cambridge, 1769. Used by permission. All rights reserved.

ISBN 13: 978-0-615-76723-9
ISBN 10: 0-615-76723-0

Cover Design: Judith McKittrick Wright

First Edition
10 11 12 13 — 9 8 7 6 5 4 3 2 1
Printed in the United States of America

Contents

Foreword ix

Prologue xiii

Chapter 1: Joan's Early Life 1

Chapter 2: Martinsville, Indiana 9

Chapter 3: Early Married Life 17

Chapter 4: Joan: Wife and Mother 23

Chapter 5: Mysterious Illness 33

Chapter 6: Myasthenia Gravis 41

Chapter 7: Counseling 51

Chapter 8: Kidney Infections 57

Chapter 9: Traumatic Events 61

Chapter 10: Joan's Wisdom 65

Chapter 11: Joan's Love 73

Chapter 12: 50th Anniversary 81

Chapter 13: Satan's Attacks 83

Chapter 14: Heavenly Peace 89

Epilogue..93

FOREWORD

I learned about the spiritual world from my mother, Joan B. W. Johnson, the "Little One," as the Lord would call her in His communications with her. My mother was, for most of her life, around five feet tall and ninety-eight pounds. She would often look at me, a six-foot-one-inch and 230-pound high-school football player and say, "How did little me ever have a big son like you?"

My mother was very sick through much of the late 1970s and 1980s with a muscular disease called myasthenia gravis. It was in the midst of some of the darkest times, when her life seemed to be very close to ending, that the Lord visited her in various ways. It started with a near-death experience which is described in detail in this book.

Then my mom had dreams and visions, and she learned to hear the Lord's still, soft voice. Much of what the Lord told my mom she wouldn't tell to just anyone because she knew it would be hard for many to believe. I believed her, and she shared almost everything the Lord showed her with me. It opened up the world of the supernatural and spiritual to me. I learned that one could be trained by the Holy Spirit to hear God's voice. Prayer is more about listening to God's voice than about telling Him what you want. Worship will draw God's presence and voice to you. Heaven is an incredible place where we will feel more alive than we ever felt on Earth. Here, Heaven seems like a dream place that is hard to comprehend, but in Heaven, the earth seems like the dream and Heaven is the wonderful reality.

I learned that I don't have to be afraid to die and, therefore, I don't have to be afraid to live on this earth, either.

My mother fought sickness in her body her whole life, but God compensated for this by speaking to her. I learned that God prefers to speak to common, everyday people. One just has to learn to listen and hear what God's Holy Spirit is saying.

My mother suffered in her body but always received comfort from Heaven. She had a way of getting through to troubled teenagers and helped many in her lifetime. Some family members couldn't believe or accept some of the incredible things that God showed my mom, so she was selective to whom she told the secrets of God. Jesus said that a prophet is never accepted in his or her own family or hometown, and my mom was aware of this. My mom told me that all messages of God, whether from her or from anyone else, can be reconciled to the Scriptures. If the message is not scriptural, then it is not from God.

When I was young, I had a learning disability, and my mom was the only one who showed any patience with me. She taught me in a way that I could grasp. Many tears and prayers went to Heaven for me from my mother. The

Lord answered my mother's prayers, and I started seeing amazing improvement in school around the fourth grade. Today, I teach college and high school history and critical-thinking classes, as well as write for magazines, articles on historical topics. I know I wouldn't be where I am today had it not been for my mom's working with and helping me. My mother's message is that God can use and speak to anyone no matter how humble the circumstances. I hope that the Holy Spirit will speak to your heart as you read my mother's life story about her incredible journey to Heaven.

—STEVEN M. JOHNSON
GREENVILLE, SOUTH CAROLINA

PROLOGUE

God had a special plan for Joan from the beginning of her life. He revealed His great plans for her through a special lady, Mrs. Brock. Later in life, God reminded Joan of Mrs. Brock's visions through a dream. In the dream, she looked down on the following scenes.

OCTOBER 5, 1980, 5:00 P.M.

When Joan was three weeks old, she was held by Mrs. Brock, Reverend Brock's wife. She was being anointed a second time by special oil, which had been saved to use on her while in front of a few elders in a small room in a special ceremony. All those present dedicated Joan to Jesus. She felt their tears on her cheeks. Earlier, she had been baptized for the first time in her parents' arms in front of the Church. Mrs. Lane and Aunt Cora, who were special people in Joan's life, also held Joan. Mrs. Brock said, "She is the one; if only we could take some of her sadness away." She foretold much sadness, loneliness, and heartache for Joan, but Joan would endure all through the help of Jesus.

THE LITTLE ONE

OCTOBER 5, 1980, 7:15 P.M.

Mrs. Brock told four-year-old Joanie to always keep the four spoons and never give them away, sell them, or tell her parents about their value. Their monetary value was not so great, but Mrs. Brock had received the spoons from special people who loved God greatly—missionaries from different parts of the world. Mrs. Brock had been told many years before that a child with child-like faith, a tiny frame, and eyes from Heaven would come to a family who would put the child through much heartache and illness. At first, she thought it would be her child, but her child had Down syndrome. She knew at Joan's baptism that she was this promised child. That morning before church, Reverend and Mrs. Brock had prayed and felt something special would happen that day. Mrs. Brock had held and baptized several babies, but knew when she held Joan that Joan was very special but would endure much hardship. As Joan grew, members of the church checked on her to make sure she was being cared for and had food to eat. Joan was in the choir at age five and could just barely see over the front choir panel. She could do anything she wanted in church.

CHAPTER 1

JOAN'S EARLY LIFE

OCTOBER 11, 1980, 10:15 P.M.

Jesus spoke to Joan in a vision:

> My Little One, your very being is love. If you give me
> your love, I give you my love. You can't out give the
> giver.
>
> You have my word that if you bring love (my name
> is Love), that when I return, it will be so joyous for all,
> because I need love, too. You can't outgive me. You
> can't love me nearly as much as I love you. Always
> make your family members, friends, and strangers
> feel special, loved.
>
> Am I a stranger? Do you fear me? Yes! Fear me
> only if you do wrong. Don't fear me; I bring you love.
> Fear is the devil's work. Satan tries to get at my Little
> One by making her sick.

Joan Beverly Webel was born March 2, 1937, to Margie
and William Webel in Saratoga Springs, New York.
Saratoga Springs was a health retreat with treatment
hotels. Flat track horse racing began in Saratoga Springs in
the late 1800s with a separate harness–racing track added

in the 1900s. Betting on the horses was a daily temptation. A huge casino for gambling was in the downtown park. By the late 1800s, Saratoga became a temporary residence for the Victorian-age wealthy during the month of August, the height of the flat track racing season. Many of the older streets in existence today are still lined with fifteen- to twenty-room mansions that are only occupied during August. The best thoroughbreds from the Kentucky Derby race at Saratoga in August. Gambling continues also.

Joan's dad, Bill, was the oldest of four sons. His father died from an accidental medical dose of poison. Bill quit school after the sixth grade and worked to support his mother and brothers. Bill and Margie fell in love and married in 1930. Bill gambled heavily, betting on the horse races and usually losing. Bill's addiction caused many problems for his family. For this reason, Joan had lived in over twenty locations by the time she was twelve years old.

Joan's reflections on her childhood express the emotional turmoil she experienced:

OCTOBER 7, 1980: 5:45 P.M.

> I remember living near an alley when I was very little. Daddy was in the alley talking to a man, and I saw a gun. Daddy promised the man, "Yeah, the money's paid. I swear on my life it's paid."
> The man answered, "I've heard that before and you were lying."

Daddy replied, "I swear—on my daughter's life—it's paid."

I knew he was lying and I was so frightened. I have always been frightened at night since then.

OCTOBER 7, 1980: 5:55 P.M.

We moved from that house that night. I look back and don't know how I lived through childhood until age twelve. Moving to Jacksonville, Florida, at age eleven was strange and done overnight—get out of town quick.

Joanie, a peacemaker, always tried so hard to smooth things over.

OCTOBER 6, 1980: 5:30 P.M.

I was four or five, and right after this, things got scary. Dad was put in jail. Mobsters came after Dad in the middle of the night with guns. I tried to give so much love and didn't ask much in return. My life was tragic. Someone in my life had crossed eyes and got special attention for it. *If my eyes were crossed, maybe they would love me,* I thought. I pretended all day that I had crossed eyes just so they would love me. They blistered me for pretending. I was a very wise child, but very open to being hurt.

I played with a girl after school in a nice home. Her parents offered to drive me home. I was embarrassed to show them where I really lived. So I told them to let me out at a doctor's house down the street. I never played with that girl again, which was my fault. At least it wasn't because of my parents or where I lived.

OCTOBER 6, 1980: 8:00 P.M.

I wore old brown shoes while other girls wore patent leather or white shoes. My socks had holes in them. My skirts were turned over to keep from being too long. My sweater sleeves came to my elbows—too big. My head didn't come to the top of the table, so tiny, the Little One. Big brown eyes, wide open—such innocence but such wisdom. The tiniest have to be courageous, because bigger ones get theirs first.

OCTOBER 6, 1980: 8:00 P.M.

How many little Joanies are there? Poor little white trash. She just wanted to be loved. She was expected to act like a grown-up. Joanie was the one that wiped Mommy's tears away when Daddy left.

I didn't know that Daddy was mad—I didn't understand drinking alcohol.

Joan took piano lessons from Blanche, whether her teacher was drunk or sober. One time, Blanche was drunk when she came to give Joan a lesson. Joan was scared and hid under the clothes in the clothes hamper.

MAY 16, 1981: 7:10 A.M.

> I would see Blanche weaving and drunk. I would help her. Blanche lived for her younger son, Tommy, and was so proud of him when he became a fireman. Tommy was killed trying a new ladder that tipped, and he fell into the flames. That was so sad.

MAY 16, 1981: 7:20 A.M.

> Mom and Dad would rent out rooms in their eighteen-room house during race month (August). Mom didn't want me around Eunice and Betty. They were prostitutes. Eunice had been a schoolteacher. One day, I was crying in the corner of the porch. Eunice asked me to sit on her lap. She was the first to teach me fractions and decimals. She was so kind to me and I loved her. Yes, she was a prostitute.

A man named Uncle Johnny rented a room from Joan's grandmother for many years. He was very kind and loved her like she was his own daughter. But he was no relation to Joanie.

MAY 16, 1981: 7:30 A.M.

I loved Uncle Johnny's relatives. They were so good
to me. Uncle Johnny cared for me and took me many,
many places.

When she was nine, Joanie was given Midge, a black
miniature Manchester terrier. Midge was Joan's best friend
for the next seventeen years.

OCTOBER 26, 1980: 6:45 A.M.

Don't fight. I didn't mean to make them mad. Midgie!
Don't kick Midgie! Let's hide in the clothes hamper.
Deeper. Midgie, I'll protect you. They're drunk. Why
did they turn the lights off? Don't hit me! Run, Midgie
run!

SEPTEMBER 25, 1980: 11:35 P.M.

A colored man, Willie, a wino, was in the gutter. I
was the littlest one and I asked him why his wrinkles
and all his scars? He pointed to every scar, "That is
because Jesus loves me." Each scar was from the war.
He said each could have killed him. All the other kids
were making fun of him until I asked him. The kids
then gathered and listened.

SEPTEMBER 25, 1980: 11:20 P.M.

> It was Jesus that gave me the ability to love. When
> I was a little girl and Uncle Francis' soldier friends
> were hurt, I would put my arms around them and
> say "hurt." I felt for that person. Biffers' Grocery—
> their son was killed in early World War II. I hugged
> him before he went to war, and cried. I knew that he
> wouldn't come back.

Joanie had a wonderful, complete love for her pets. In October 1946, her dad won a turkey in a drawing. She was nine. Her dad put the turkey in a cage in the spare room. Joanie named her Peggy and faithfully fed the turkey every day as her pet.

For Thanksgiving, the family was expecting a lot of company. Joanie's mom fixed a huge dinner. When Joanie walked into the dining room, she saw Peggy in the middle of the table. She cried out, "Peggy!" and ran crying from the room. Joanie didn't eat that day. Dinner was delayed a little until the others recovered from her terrible discovery. Peggy disappeared that day. "Poor Peggy!" Joanie cried.

CHAPTER 2

MARTINSVILLE, INDIANA

Joan's uncle, Harry Herz, who lived in Chicago, bought a lumber mill in the small town of Martinsville, Indiana (population 5,000), in early 1950. He and Aunt Harriet moved to Martinsville. He needed a manager for the sawmill, so he offered the job to his brother-in-law, Bill Webel. Bill accepted and moved his family to the farming community from Saratoga Springs, New York. Joan had just turned thirteen. She entered Mrs. Silvia Smith's sixth grade class at Central Elementary School for the last six weeks of the school year. There was no gambling for Bill in Martinsville.

Judy, who became Joan's best friend, lived a few houses away from her. They rode bicycles around their neighborhood. During the summer, they rode their bikes past my house. I always seemed to be reading a book in the dining room rocking chair when they passed. Judy called me "The Book Worm." Later that summer, I was in the side yard when the girls rode by. I remember, just like it was yesterday, meeting Joan for the first time.

Joan and I went to seventh grade parties and played spin-the-bottle and other games. That resulted in my first kiss with Joanie. We talked on the phone often, which was strange because I couldn't do that with any other girl. I was tongue-tied!

Joan had many friends in school, both girls and boys. She was always friendly, kind, and smiling. Even then, we could see the love of the Lord through Joanie.

My best friend in seventh and eighth grade was Tom, who lived two blocks away. Joan started dating Tom, and they went steady together in the eighth and ninth grades. Tom's family really liked Joan. Then Tom's father, who was a manager of the Sears store and was a big man, had a sudden heart attack and died. Tom and his whole family were devastated.

Joan spent a lot of time with Tom and his family. She was very loving, caring, and helpful to them during their deep sorrow and loss. In looking back, the Lord placed Joan there to help Tom and his family through that terrible, sorrowful time.

But Joan's stress at home continued . . .

JULY 16, 1981: 7:10 A.M.

> Paul worked for Daddy at the lumber mill. He was drunk. Daddy wouldn't pay him until he sobered up. Paul pulled an eight-inch knife and had Daddy against the wall with the knife to his neck. Daddy's men saw through the office window and overpowered Paul. He was a cousin to John Dillinger, a 1930s murderer and bank robber, who had lived ten miles away. Daddy was always good to Paul.

After the ninth grade, Joan's father received a job offer—one that promised to pay well—to return to Saratoga Springs and hang delicate wall paper in the new Skidmore College dormitory buildings. He accepted and Joan and her parents moved back to Saratoga Springs, against Joan's tearful objections. At Joan's going-away party, although she was still going steady with Tom, I got in Joan's going-away kissing line for the boys and received two good-bye kisses.

Joan really missed Martinsville. She had her dad wallpaper her room black with red trim—depressing. She and Tom wrote regularly back and forth. But Tom started dating Judy (not the Judy who was Joan's best friend) after about six months, and they started going steady. Joan's sophomore year in New York was lonely and depressing. Her parents agreed to let her return to Martinsville for her junior year. She lived with her married sister.

I remember, like it was yesterday, the first time I saw Joan after she came back. I was working at Kroger's, stocking jelly and peanut butter on the shelves beside the dairy case in the store's back aisle. She came in to talk but had with her this big handsome boy she introduced as Danny. I thought, "Nuts! She brought a boyfriend back with her." I learned several weeks later that Danny was her cousin.

Within two weeks, I had asked Joan for a date. By November of our junior year, we were going steady. The only uncertain time was in December of our senior year when we broke up to date others. It was Joan's idea. Taking Joan's best friend Sharon's advice, I asked Carolyn for a date to go to Indianapolis to see the Bing Crosby movie, *White Christmas*. That really made Joan jealous and neither one of us dated anyone else again.

"That is what made me realize my love for my Bill," Joan said. Joan never wanted to see *White Christmas* because of who I took to see the movie.

After returning to Martinsville, Joanie was with all of her previous friends. She went to many slumber parties, ball games, and dances. Joan was happy in school and did well in her classes. In 4-H, she once baked an angel food cake that fell flat. So she took a purchased angel food cake to the fair and received a first-place blue ribbon. Would Jesus have approved that?

Joan and I had great times at the junior and senior proms. Every Wednesday night during the summer between our junior and senior years, we went to the Westlake open-air dance pavilion located on the south side of Indianapolis. We danced to big-name bands, and I was in "7th Heaven" hearing them play. We saw Stan Kenton, Billy May, the Dorsey Brothers, Glen Miller, and other bands. These were one-night-only events, as they would go on to play in Chicago the next night. I knew that would be no life for me—although I was an excellent clarinet player—in a dance band while also a married or family man.

During her senior year, Joan's parents moved back to Martinsville. They were excellent parents in Martinsville because they were away from the gambling and heavy drinking. They raised registered English Pug puppies and sold them. Joan became a car-hop at the local A&W Root Beer stand and saved her money. Her most infamous root beer delivery was to a Cadillac with four men in white suits seated inside. She tripped on her roller skates and dumped the large root beers onto the men in the front seat. No more roller skates after that for Joan!

I went to Wabash College as a freshman on a scholarship. I had to maintain a *B* average to keep my scholarship. I was nervous about my grades and studied all of the time. The only time I relaxed that year was when I was with Joan on the weekends. We became engaged on Joan's birthday, March 2, 1957. With my parents' agreement, we intended to get married during the summer of 1959.

After high school, Joan entered beautician school in Indianapolis. After graduating in May 1957, she went to work for Mabel's salon in Martinsville.

During the summer before my sophomore year, I dreaded more and more going back to college. Then, on Saturday night, August 17, 1957, with my dance band playing as we danced, I asked Joan to marry me on Sunday, August 25.

My parents severely objected to our getting married. My dad's concluding statement was, "If you go ahead and do this, I will cut you off without a cent!" After that statement, I would have dug ditches before asking my dad for a penny. So we were married on August 25 by Reverend Raphael in the Presbyterian Church. None of my family attended. A few years later, my mother admitted that her greatest life's regret was missing our wedding.

There is no doubt our match was made in Heaven! The Lord brought Joan from Saratoga Springs, 900 miles away, to small-town Martinsville to be my wife. Thank you, Lord, for blessing my life with your special child, Joanie.

SEPTEMBER 27, 1980: 9:35 A.M.

> We are able to take things selfishly but somehow slough it off or rationalize it. When the whole universe and eternity are given to us, we are suspicious of God and resist. We complicate life when life must stay simple in the Lord. We take wages from work because we earned them. But the Lord gives freely and we are suspicious; what's the catch? We know that we are doing right by the blessings that we receive inside and outside. Inner peace; and we do not fear the future.

CHAPTER 3

EARLY MARRIED LIFE

J oanie's only dowry was her two dogs: Midgie, her best friend since the age of nine, and a handsome, lovable, three-year-old pug who was not real smart. They were our first kids.

Our first home at Wabash College was half of a former World War II tin Quonset hut. Our college addition was called "Mud Hollow." It was our love home, except when the termites swarmed in the spring.

I would study late at night. Joanie would go to bed with a string tied around my big toe. When she woke up, she pulled the string. If I didn't pull back, she woke me up and took me to bed.

We looked for our first Christmas tree before they were even selling them. We put all blue lights on it; some of the blue paint flaked off and showed white light through. It was beautiful! We enjoyed it every night. However, all of the needles had fallen off the tree by Christmas.

Joan's parents helped us all of the time at Mud Hollow. Our first winter, the oil heater didn't work. Joan's dad spent over $500 on a new oil heater and installed it. They also came over every couple of weeks, and her dad always slipped me a twenty dollar bill. They loved me like I was their own son. They did not have very much money, but they shared what they had.

After my sophomore year, we moved back to Martinsville to live with Joan's parents. Joan was three months pregnant and the lifting during the move caused her to have a miscarriage. She was in the Martinsville hospital for ten days because the doctors could not get the bleeding to stop. She learned to hate apricots because the hospital fed them to her every day.

Then Pugs began struggling to breathe and passing out, particularly on hot days. We had no money, but we took Pugs to the vet to determine what was wrong. The vet took Pugs's tonsils out for $175 and Pugs could breathe much better. We paid the vet's bill over many months.

Joanie had taught Midgie many tricks. One day in Mud Hollow, Joan had Midgie stand on her hind legs by our sofa. She then went across the street to visit with a neighbor. When she came back, Midgie was still standing on her hind legs. Joanie told Midgie to sit down. I didn't mind *that* well! I blew up our first ten-dollar television when I spilled Pepsi down it. I bought a better TV for fifteen dollars. Joan was scanning the TV channels one day in July when she found a program on which people were singing Christmas Carols. She stopped to watch. It was Ruth Lyons' daily hour-and-a-half show on WLW-TV from Cincinnati. Joan watched every day after that. Ruth was very positive and "down-to-earth" as she talked with her excellent guests. After college, we got tickets to be on the live Ruth Lyons show. Each time we went, Joan filled out a card before the show started. Her card was always picked to be interviewed by Ruth on the live show. Her first card commented that she had first watched Ruth in July singing Christmas Carols.

My two best friends from my freshman year, Jack and Milt, spent lots of time at our Quonset hut, even when I wasn't there. Joan was best friends with them also— talking with, listening to, and feeding them.

Ray and Joann lived in the other half of our Quonset hut during my junior year. They both spent a lot of time at our place with Joan, who was friendly and always had coffee available. I would come home from afternoon chemistry labs and have to step over six-foot-five-inch Ray's long legs stretched across our narrow living room. They were great friends because of Joan's love for others.

During our senior year, Joan became pregnant and the doctor said she was due November 15, 1959. I told my classmates that I might have to leave on short notice to get my wife to the hospital. However, by December 1, I was tired of answering questions about whether or not the baby had been born. Our baby was finally born on December 17, 1959. Joanie had a normal delivery. Our daughter, Janet Lynn, had light red hair and was in perfect health. My mother came to help Joan with the baby after they got home. The baby awoke at 1 a.m. for feeding. I was still studying, so I got up to feed Jan. Mom also got up to feed her. We wanted Joan to rest and sleep. Mom and I had a tug-of-war over who was going to feed Jan. Joan finally got up, took Jan, and fed her. Mom packed up and left the next morning!

Joan was a member of the Dames Club, which was a group of students' wives. One day, the Dames Club went bowling. On Joan's first turn, she swung her arm backward and dropped the bowling ball. It rolled back toward the girls. After that, the girls would not stand or sit behind her. She was still the "little one" at five feet tall and 105 pounds.

I graduated from Wabash College on June 1, 1960. I had taken a project engineer's job with General Motors Corporation and we moved to Anderson, Indiana. For the previous six years, I had played clarinet to lead a four-piece dance band on most Saturday nights. Joan had been a wallflower at many of these dances. After graduation, I promised to put up the clarinet and we would dance together.

CHAPTER 4

JOAN: WIFE AND MOTHER

Six months after I was hired at General Motors, more engineering graduates were interviewed. I was asked to give each one a plant tour. Joan was asked to show each of their wives around Anderson, which was strange because Joan did not know Anderson very well! We also took each couple to dinner that same evening.

The first couple we met was Don and Sandy. For Sandy's tour, Joan began by driving up and down the street next to the courthouse square, which had six or seven dingy-looking bars on it. She then showed Sandy the worst parts of Anderson. We laughed about it at dinner. However, Don took the job and we have been best friends since that day.

The second couple we met was Chris and Carol. Joan also showed Carol the worst parts of Anderson. She even drove the wrong way down a one-way street. Afterward, Chris and Carol visited our house. As we talked about the day, Carol slipped off her chair and landed on the floor. We laughed about it at dinner. Chris took the job and we, too, have been best friends since.

Don, Chris, and I joined the Elks Club. We started going to their dances every Saturday night. We all loved to dance and had great times together. We thought the Elks Club had a strange ceremony, though. At 11:00 p.m. every Saturday night, the Exalted Ruler would solemnly say into the microphone, "Now we will memorialize our dear departed brothers. Wherever an elk may roam. . . ." It was our misbehaving wives!

One night, Sandy looked at Joan and they started giggling very hard. They both slipped off their chairs and fell under the table. We husbands were so embarrassed! Not really.

We went out to dinner with friends every weekend. We played in couples' Bridge Club every two weeks with our best friends. Joan played in the ladies' Bridge Club every two weeks.

One year after I started working for General Motors, we bought our first house. It was our dream home; a three-bedroom, white frame home with red roses on a trellis on either side of the front porch entrance.

We needed the space, as our child was growing up quickly. When Jan was two-and-a-half years old, Joan and I took her shopping in the Sears basement store on a Friday night in 1962. At one point, Joan looked down and asked, "Do you have Jan with you?"

"I thought you had her," I replied.

We both were scared and started looking all over for Jan. I am very tall and finally spotted her coat through the crowd.

"Joan," I called, "I see her by that bunch of people. Get Jan quick!"

Joan was laughing so hard that tears were running down her face. Finally she giggled, "She is your daughter. *You* get her!"

I went through the crowd. Very quietly, I whispered, "No, no Jan! We don't use the toilet in the bathroom display in front of people."

Jan kept saying, "But Daddy, I've got to go!" The big crowd was laughing.

Trying to act normal, I said, "Honey, help Daddy get you dressed again."

Little Jan was so proud. She said to everyone, "Good girl! Good girl! Daddy, you proud? Me not go in pretty panties!"

Joanie delivered three healthy, strong babies in July 1963, October 1965, and October 1967. We were surprised that our first son, Steve, born in July 1963, had lots of black hair. He had solid black hair between his head and eyebrows and black hair on his shoulders. I was hurt that Joan, after first seeing him, said, "He's not very pretty!"

"He's beautiful—our first son!" I retorted back to her. Fortunately, the hair above his eyebrows and on his shoulders fell off after the first day.

Before Joan delivered our second daughter, Lisa, in October 1965, we commented that a plumber had just been in Joan's room. Her dad said, "Maybe he had heard that her water broke!"

Before our youngest son, Michael, was born in October 1967, Joan's heavy labor started at 5 a.m. It took me until 6:30 a.m. to get the babysitter for our three kids and get Joan into the car. By then, she was taking deep breaths and saying the baby was very close to birth. I told her to relax. I wasn't worried. I dropped her off at the back of the hospital at 6:55 a.m. I was parked and at the nurse's desk at 7 a.m. I told the desk clerk who I was. She said, "Congratulations! You have a son!"

After each baby, I gave Joan three or four weeks to recover. I then expected her to resume her duties of changing diapers, fixing three meals per day, doing the laundry, cleaning the house, and completely resuming our social activities. I was preoccupied with climbing the promotion ladder at General Motors and achieving business success. Each of our four children attended Sunday school and church youth activities every Sunday as soon as they were old enough.

SEPTEMBER 27, 1980: 9:35 A.M

"Jesus said, 'To be an infant in God is a wonderful thing'—not embarrassing. For Jesus loved the little children. Once an infant is in Christ, growth can come so fast. The right answers will be so much easier to receive. He has given us gifts of our world: our children. We must be willing to give up even each other. Bill, don't be jealous of Joan; this is Satanic. Don't be jealous of what Joan has because you can have this, too."

OCTOBER 11, 1980: 10:30 P.M.

All things are possible through God. Our God is such a good God. Another way to spell "Love" is J-E-S-U-S.

Our second vacation to Florida was in 1965 to Sarasota. We left our kids with their grandparents. Our first night was at a Howard Johnson Motel. The next morning we met our friends, Don and Sandy, at the Frontenac Motel on the ocean. Don and I were going to play golf. Joan and Sandy, who was kind of obsessed about getting a suntan, planned to get some sun on the beach. However, the weather that day stayed below sixty degrees Fahrenheit with a strong breeze, in spite of a full sun.

Don and I wore short pants. As soon as we got out of our car at the golf course, an obvious Florida native asked us, "Where are you from? Up North?" My knees turned blue from the cold air that day.

When we returned to the Frontenac, we discovered Joan and Sandy were still lying on the beach in front of a wall that blocked the wind. Both had worn coats over their swimming suits, lain down on the reclining chairs, and opened up their coats. Joan had a sunburn on top of her goose bumps!

While I was growing up in Martinsville, Indiana, Mom and Dad would always take a week-long vacation to Silver Lake, which was forty to fifty miles north of Muskegon, Michigan. Silver Lake had sand dunes between it and Lake Michigan; the dunes were approximately five miles long and four miles wide—one giant sand pile to play in!

The sun sets beautifully over the sand dunes and lake. We were always on the opposite side of the lake where the white sandy beaches went out into the water for fifty yards to a maximum depth of four feet. We enjoyed swimming and lots of good fishing.

I finally persuaded Joan to take our one-week family vacation at Silver Lake in late August 1968. The cabin that I rented was the same one my family had used fifteen years earlier. The broken, dirty sofas and chairs; the outhouse out back; and the early American kitchen were unchanged. Joan's previous experience with vacations had been nice motels and meals purchased out.

Being late August, the warmest temperature that week was sixty degrees Fahrenheit. However, we could not get the oil heater working for the first two or three days. Joan spent the first two days cleaning the sand from previous tenants out of the cabin. She cried herself to sleep for at least the first two nights.

Joan's main job was to care for and feed ten-month-old baby Michael. For the rest of our three older children: Jan, age nine; Steve, age five; and Lisa, age three; I had big plans each day—even in fifty- to sixty-degree weather. One day, we took the rowboat and went up the lake inlet (the lake diameter was probably four miles). The next day, we took the rowboat and went up the lake outlet (the other side of the lake) to Lake Michigan. We spent a couple of days playing on the sand dunes and even included a dune ride. We did some fishing and wading since the water was too cold for swimming. Together, we watched sunsets over the sand dunes every night and had cookouts and fires outside to warm us in the evenings

The three older children and I did everything I had fun doing at Silver Lake as a kid. It was like a second childhood for me. We had a ball. But Joan didn't! On the way home, we all talked about our great time—everyone, that is, except Joan. I became afraid we would never see the place again, but Joan said she would only go back if we had a decent place, not a dump, to stay in. Hallelujah!

The next July, I rented a large log cabin (1,500 square feet) with two bedrooms, a large living room with a fireplace, and a nice kitchen. This rental cabin cost a lot more than the previous summer's house. Two of our best friends lived in Milwaukee and took a huge ferry boat with their car on board to Muskegon. They stayed with us in our Silver Lake log cabin for a couple of days and then went back to Milwaukee on the ferry boat.

Joan and I drove to Muskegon to see them off. We were a little late and I was rushing ahead of Joan. Soon, we were separated by the freight cars being loaded onto the ferry boat. So Joan turned around and walked back to our car. Four-foot-tall weeds in a ten-foot-wide field separated the parking lot from the water. A man was lying in the weeds, waiting. He jumped on little five-foot-tall Joan, pulled her into the weeds, and got on top of her. He was intent on raping her. Fortunately, she had our camera on a band around her right wrist. She swung the camera as hard as she could into his eye, hoping to put it out. He jumped off her in great pain and took off. She crawled back to the car and was cowering down on the floor of the front seat, in tears and frightened, when I found her. We reported the incident to the police. Two days later, she was still frightened and we went home a day early. The Lord had protected Joan from rape, and maybe death, by helping her stay calm and have the camera as a weapon.

Joan and I enjoyed our four children as they grew up. We took them to zoos, parks, watched them play sports, and went to Florida every spring for vacation at Sarasota and Sanibel Island beaches, Disney World, Universal Studios, and Busch Gardens.

Our best-ever family vacation was our 1973 spring trip. We drove to Sarasota and stayed at the Frontenac Motel on the Gulf of Mexico for eight days. The weather was eighty-two degrees and sunny every day. Joan lay out in the sun. I played with our four children in the Gulf. We rode the waves for hours. We could go out fifty yards and the water came up only to my chest. We had an air-inflated raft with paddles and air mattresses. We took showers to get the salt off and finished our fun in the swimming pool. Every evening, we watched a beautiful sunset over the Gulf.

Next, we drove to Disney World and stayed three nights and four days in a suite on the top floor of the Contemporary Hotel. We looked like gypsies because our kids carried their clothes in large paper bags.

When we walked into our room, Joan giggled for thirty minutes in disbelief at our amazing room. The living room was twenty-five feet by forty feet across with two balconies overlooking the Magic Kingdom. A full kitchen and dining area were located at the back of this large room. We had a separate bedroom with two full-size beds and a bathroom.

We had tickets to all of the attractions at Magic Kingdom and rode each attraction several times. Every night, we watched the fireworks from our room's balcony. We rented a boat and rode around the lake and swam at the beach beside the hotel. A month after driving home, we were still smiling from the joy of our great vacation.

CHAPTER 5

MYSTERIOUS ILLNESS

Throughout the years when Joan was having babies and resuming her duties as homemaker, social companion, mother, and wife, she kept getting weaker. But I was too busy with work to see it. Joanie never complained or asked for help. She just kept smiling.

Finally, I noticed Joanie was napping more and more when I got home from work. Her housework would not be finished. Her only answer was "tired." Then I started finding partially empty liquor bottles hidden in the clothes hamper and her dresser drawers. I asked her if she had been drinking. Her answer was "Yes, just to relax." I told her this had to stop, but she continued.

We put her in an alcoholic recovery hospital in Indianapolis for two weeks. She came home sober. But I didn't reduce her workload by helping her or hiring a helper. She started drinking again. I put her back in an alcoholic recovery hospital for two weeks. We also joined

Alcoholics Anonymous and Al-Anon, the group for spouses, and attended the weekly meetings.

Then Joan wrecked our station wagon with our youngest child in the front seat. She had been drinking and hit a telephone pole. Our child was fine, but Joan mashed her nose and needed it reconstructed.

She seemed to be drifting back into the alcoholism. Then she called me into our room to tell me she had taken a whole bottle of sleeping pills so she could end it all. She would not be an embarrassment anymore.

I carried her to the hospital. I sat up all night with her and prayed that the Lord wouldn't take her yet. The children and I loved her and needed her so much. She was the love of my life.

That night, Joan had a near-death experience. She said, "I floated above my body and into the light. I was going toward an object; it was Midgie, my best-friend dog from my teen years. I picked up Midgie and Midgie kissed me. I then saw Jesus. He said, 'It is not your time yet, Little One, but I keep those things most precious to you here for you in Heaven.'

"As I looked around at the beauty of Heaven, Jesus said to me, 'Come, Little One. I will let you look into Heaven but not enter in yet.'

"He opened the gate. Before me was the Kingdom of Heaven in all its magnificence. I saw gardens and flowers and smelled fragrances like I never had experienced before. Music came from everywhere, unlike any sound on earth, but stirring to the soul. Far to the left was a crystal sea with boats on it. To the right were mountains and a lake of breathtaking beauty. Far away in the middle of the scene, on top of a large mountain, was a building. It was the throne room of God. Flowing from the mountain to the gate was the River of Life.

"Jesus said, 'In Heaven, you will remember all events from earth. You will wash in the River of Life and wash away the pain and hurt associated with life. Don't fear death. This will be waiting for you. You must go back now. Visiting Heaven this way seems like a dream. When you are really here in Heaven, this will be so real and invigorating. Life in your past world will then seem like a dream.'

"I woke up the next morning bright-eyed, smiling, and ready to go. I said, 'I felt like a new life was starting for me.' The Lord had given me a miracle healing."

OCTOBER 11, 1980: 10:30 P.M.

I had to die to find out how to live.

Joan still had too many lives to change and too much to do. Thank you, Lord, for keeping Joanie with us! They kept her in the hospital for two weeks for observation and then released her. Joan never drank any alcohol again.

But the weakness and tiredness continued.

The Little One

October 5, 1980: 4:45 P.M.

After a few visits to a new doctor, the doctor would conclude that I was too sensitive. I could not take the pressure of the world and my family. He would refer me to a psychiatrist. Tranquilizers would then be prescribed. Two doctors actually prescribed that I take alcoholic drinks to relax me. No wonder I was nervous. For years, doctors told me that nothing was wrong with me. I knew that something was wrong and responsible for my weakness.

Our oldest son, Steve, failed the first grade. He was the biggest child in his class, but a slower learner. His first grade teacher called him "dumb" and "stupid." He retook first grade with another teacher. Joanie worked with him on his homework every night, encouraged him, and prayed with him. He steadily improved during his second first grade class and got much better grades. But, he still had the reputation of being big and dumb in that school. So we moved and changed school districts. In the fourth grade, he received *B*'s and *C*'s and continued doing better in school. Now, he has a master's degree and teaches high school and college history. He has been rated by his supervisors and students as one of the college's best, most interesting, and effective teachers. He owes it all to his mother's and Jesus' patient and loving instruction.

Steve has also written four long magazine articles about famous empires and battles around the world. The *Strategy and Tactics* magazine has accepted and approved those articles for publication. He owes it all to his mother's and Jesus' patient and loving instruction.

JANUARY 17, 1981: 9:15 P.M.

> For unto you is born a son, and he shall be called Emmanuel (Steven) (meaning "God is with us"). He is strong and to be a protector and teacher. He was dumb, but now he is very smart.

Joan taught Steve that Jesus Christ is his best friend:

> Plead the blood of Jesus. Talk to Jesus and he will lead you and help you.
>
> A birthday is a gift from God. Another year to grow, a chance to learn the wondrous things God feels we should know. It's like a new adventure, full of places not yet seen, full of people we can meet, and dreams we've yet to dream. It's like a new awakening, a search for who we are. If we seek in earnest the empty hole in our life, our discoveries take us far beyond any man's dream. When we put our best into each moment we live, then we are truly giving God the best thanks we can give.

All of our children were raised in church as Christians. The churches we selected had the most loving and entertaining programs and teachers for our children as they grew. Joanie told our children, "Jesus loves you. So do I. . . . I love you so very much. . . . Today is the first day of the rest of your life. . . . If God is for us, who can be against us? . . . You can hear God's voice. But sometimes we have static or interference and can't hear God. Listen for the still small voice of the Lord. . . . We are not allowed to be bored—so never use that word."

When Lisa was depressed, Joan would tell her, "Poor Lisa. Go eat worms!" This would always make Lisa smile and get her out of her depression. And no, she sure wasn't going to eat worms!

Lisa fondly remembers Joanie's favorite things were Jesus, Dad, her kids, beautiful clothes, silver and gold shoes, beautiful jewelry, green eye shadow, her spoon collection, the TV show "Murder She Wrote," and huge purses in which she couldn't find her driver's license to show to the policeman.

We talked about adopting two more children after our four were grown up. However, we stopped talking about this when Steve, Lisa, and Michael were all teenagers at the same time and causing problems. Joan was sick during much of this time. Our two youngest, Lisa and Michael, were rebellious and left home after their high school graduations. They admitted they wanted to get away from Joan's constant illness and our constant prayers for Joan's healing. Michael felt that one prayer should have healed her. Thankfully, we would later learn that the Lord remembered how we wanted two more young children to raise.

Finally, in September 1976, we began finding answers about Joan's illness after she read an article about myasthenia gravis, a strength-robbing disease. Dr. Tee, the article's author, had devoted his medical career to studying this disease. And he lived in Indianapolis, only thirty-five miles from our home.

CHAPTER 6

MYASTHENIA GRAVIS

THIS CHAPTER IS COMPOSED OF JOAN'S WORDS, WRITTEN ON SUNDAY, APRIL 6, 1977.

I feel so full of life this morning! I have to share happiness because it is easy to find if you really try. My family just left for church. I wish I could be with them, but I've been ill and in bed for several months. I have myasthenia gravis.

Even as I lie in bed today, it is hard for me to think of myself as being handicapped. I have seen and heard of many handicapped people for whom I felt so sorry I could cry for them. I never thought that it could, or would, hit me, Joan Johnson. I have myasthenia gravis—I could die from this! Me! My mind works perfectly. I can laugh and cry. I can hear people talking about me. And when I hear what they say, I feel as if they are talking about a tragic, pitiful person I do not know.

Imagine having this dreadful disease for over ten years before someone would believe that something was wrong with me. I wonder how many people have a real disease that so weakens their bodies that they feel guilty, angry, and frustrated until they finally give up life. These tragedies and frustrations are magnified because no one thinks you are sick: only lazy, mentally ill, or an alcoholic, and much more.

Reread what I have just told you! I am talking about myself. But this could happen to you, too! Wake up!

If I am scaring you, I am sorry! But do you really listen to your loved ones? If your loved one has an illness, do not make her feel that she is a bad, sinful person, because the Devil may have taken her health, mind, or strength away! Every illness in the world today could be less tragic if all people would quit judging.

My four great children, wonderful husband, and I have gone through some really bad times. We did not know how ill I was. God has saved my life so many times! Thank you, Lord!

It must seem strange to most people, but I am so grateful and feel fortunate to finally find out there is hope for me. I will be almost normal very soon! You see, I had been weak for many years. At times I did not have enough strength to drag myself to the kitchen . . .

FLASHBACK

> I'm so tired. How can I do those dishes? I can't walk
> to the sink. I'm too tired to get to the couch to lie
> down. I'll just lie here on the floor to rest. Everyone
> thinks I'm drinking, but I'm not!

Sometimes getting dressed would wear me out for the entire day. At times, I have had severe pain throughout my body and blinding headaches. I have gone to doctors for years trying to find out the causes. After the doctors couldn't find a medical reason, they usually said my problem was nerves . . . mental! Nerves—baloney!

FLASHBACK (TWELVE YEARS EARLIER)

> Dr. Joe, I don't drink too much. I'm just weak. I can't
> walk straight and I'm not drinking. I go to look and
> my eyes don't focus. Can't you hear me? I speak and
> no one hears. Dr. Joe, it's not in my head! I don't need
> a psychiatrist!

Bill and I have felt that there had to be medical reasons. And why shouldn't I be nervous, too? I'm too weak to take care of my family and to go and do things with them. I have not known what was wrong with me for years. The pain in my heart has been almost worse than the pain in my body. Guilt! Guilt! Guilt! Doctors—Psychiatrists—telling me all of this is in my head! I wonder how many people have gone crazy because of illnesses they didn't know they had.

Seven months ago, I became so weak I had to stay in bed all of the time. At times I had double vision, or my vision would blur with half-opened eyes. I also had a thick tongue and slurred speech. I was having great difficulty swallowing and breathing. My throat felt like it was closing.

FLASHBACK

> Bill, Bill, I can't move! Turn me over on my side. I can't hold my head up. I ache all over. My chest hurts— pressure on my chest. It's hard to breathe. I can't get my breath—my throat is closing. My voice is going— can't ta . . . ta . . . alk . . .

My neck muscles were very weak. Sometimes I couldn't hold my head up. In July 1976, nine months ago, I joined a health spa to exercise and try to build up my strength. One day, I did neck muscle exercises at the spa. Afterwards, I couldn't hold my head up and I haven't been the same since. I was also frequently experiencing severe bowel blockage.

I went to our family doctor, Dr. Beg, three times in September and October 1976 for more tests. I also read an article about myasthenia gravis during that time and discovered its symptoms sound like mine. I questioned Dr. Beg about myasthenia gravis. He said that he didn't know much about it, except that there is no cure for it and people generally die from it. I asked him about Dr. Tee, a world-renowned doctor in Indianapolis, only thirty-five miles away. He was an expert in this disease and had written the article. Dr. Beg said that Dr. Tee didn't take many patients. I probably wouldn't be able to get in to see him. Dr. Beg still felt that it was all in my head and had given up on me!

I wrote a letter to Dr. Tee describing my symptoms and asking for help. I was able to get an appointment that I'll never forget—on December 21, 1976! Dr. Tee was very kind as we discussed my symptoms. He tested my hand and neck muscle strength and found that I was very weak. He then injected Tensilon into my arm and repeated the previous tests. My strength had remarkably increased this time. Dr. Tee explained to Bill and me that I had a fairly severe case of myasthenia gravis. He further explained that this disease is an extreme weakness of the muscles and is caused by a breakdown in the signal the nerve endings send to my muscles to contract or expand. As a result, I may want my muscles to do something, but they won't work; or they respond weakly or slowly. The cause and cure of the disease are unknown. Medicine can be taken to help restore the patient to almost normal functioning; just like insulin helps a diabetic. The medicine helps restore the chemical balance between the nerve ends and muscles so that normal muscular action can take place. The key was to find the correct chemical, out of four options available, and the proper dosage for my system.

Dr. Tee said that in 1935, over ninety percent of the myasthenia gravis diagnosed patients died from total inability to breathe or handle their secretions. Today (1977), more than ninety percent survive, with many able to do useful work. It is estimated that as many as 500,000 cases of myasthenia gravis are still undiagnosed in this country due to lack of knowledge about the disease by the general public or doctors. I was thankful and relieved to finally know what I was fighting. Dr. Tee gave me further hope by stating that some of his patients with my severity of myasthenia gravis had undergone remission after a period of time on the proper medication.

After some trial and error, my medication and dosage were set, after approximately two months. Much of my strength had been restored although I did not have any endurance. I tired quickly. The medicine dosage level was extremely high. Excessive dosage could cause severe reactions: twitching eyes and mouth, severe muscle cramping, vomiting, throat closing, and death! I had antidote tablets with me at all times in case of an overdose. My degree of weakness varied somewhat from day to day; therefore my dosage varied from day to day.

My family, many of my friends, and our church continued to encourage, help, and pray for me. Reverend Bob Shearer, our minister, spent hours with me in our home teaching patience to me and praying with me for healing. I knew that Jesus had forgiven my sins. Now I had to forgive myself and like myself a little. God loves me as much as anyone else!

In the past eight years, God has gotten me through three major auto accidents, two nose surgery operations, internal cysts, infectious hepatitis, scarlet fever, and now . . . myasthenia gravis. God has pulled me through all of these things and I know that God wants my body and mind well! All I had to do now was be happy and believe that, in time, God would heal me completely. I believe that a mental change had to come, just as much as physical health to my body.

I have been watching Reverend Oral Roberts on television for several months. He has had a positive effect upon me which is amazing. He has also had a lot to do with my planting of seeds of faith and watching them grow! And he helped me believe a healing miracle would happen to me. It did!

Approximately six weeks ago, I was strong enough to write a sympathy note to Rev. Roberts. In the note, I prayed that God would give him and his family strength to endure the tragic loss of his daughter and son-in-law who were killed in an airplane crash. Two weeks later, I received a telephone call. The voice said, "Hello Mrs. Johnson. This is Oral Roberts."

I replied, "Sure you're Oral Roberts; and I'm Billy Graham! Who is this? I know you're playing a joke." It took Rev. Roberts a minute to convince me that I was really talking to him. My mouth dropped open and I was trembling.

Rev. Roberts continued, "Thank you for your card and prayers, Joan. And you didn't even ask to be prayed for. You were praying for me. Your card has laid on my desk for three days. I haven't been able to pass it to my secretary. I have reread it several times. I feel that you also have a burden. You didn't say so in your letter. Can I pray for you?"

I told Rev. Roberts about my myasthenia gravis. He replied, "My dear Joan, Jesus loves you. And I do, too. I believe a miracle is going to happen to you today!"

Rev. Roberts then prayed a special prayer that I could feel from the top of my head to the tips of my toes! "Dear God, my partners have given tremendous help to Evelyn, Richard, myself, and the rest of my family. And the cards and letters that have been sent have helped so much. I would like to call and touch every partner. But your beautiful expression, Joan, like God is speaking through you, gave me special peace. And I had to thank you personally. Now God, my dear partner, Mrs. Johnson, has a burden on her heart.

"God has a miracle for you! You have been ill and your life has been filled with tragedies. It was not the will of God for you to have this now. Through your faith in Jesus Christ and all that Jesus had suffered for, I expect a miracle to happen in your healing! I feel a kind of bravery in you that only God's people have. I pray that you do not have bitterness over your problems. Through your faith, in Jesus' name, *God will heal you!*"

He asked, "Are you healed?"

"Yes, I know I am!"

"Who healed you?"

"Jesus Christ!"

"Praise God!"

Today, April 6, one month after this phone call, I am on my feet and getting stronger each day! As a measure of my faith, I threw my myasthenia gravis medicine away after the phone call. Now I am really alive and enjoying everything! I have a great flash of excitement each day; particularly when I can help someone understand what I know! By giving, I get so much more than I ever give.

My life has just begun! Bill and I have a closeness that only God could place between us. It is truly God's love and blessing! The Lord has given me another miracle with which my life was saved.

CHAPTER 7

COUNSELING

1977

> The greatest talent God gave me is the ability to actu-
> ally feel one's pain or happiness. I knew exactly the
> inner feelings of people. I have lived so many different
> lives in so many different ways. I pray that I can pass
> this wisdom and love to as many people and chil-
> dren that my health and lifetime will permit. I am so
> thankful for my sensitivity for all. I have been able to
> use my own disabilities, weaknesses, and other quali-
> ties, good or bad, to the Lord's advantage.

Tom, whom we knew in Martinsville, also lived in
Anderson. He was with an organization that helped
troubled teenage girls who were depressed, pregnant,
angry, or in trouble with the police. He knew Joan had a
loving, kind, and understanding heart and asked her to
counsel the girls. So she met with them in the afternoons
while I was at work. I knew when she had been counseling
because she was mentally exhausted when I got home.

Joan was very successful at helping sixty-three teenage
girls straighten out their thinking and attitudes. But, after

one committed suicide, she stopped counseling. She felt she had somehow failed.

> The more you can love, the less you can hate. If love is in your heart, you can win anyone with true love and patience.

Around this time, I talked to a father at our church; he was having rebellion problems with his oldest son, Ken. Ken had been making straight *A*'s but was now failing. He had become increasingly hard to live with as he was a threat to the family's two younger children. He had literally threatened to kill his little sister. Counselors had not been able to help. The family was seriously considering sending Ken away.

Ken's father and mother were stiff and unfeeling. I told his father about Joan's great success in counseling troubled teenage girls. Could Joan try with Ken? They agreed. Ken and our son Steve were both juniors in high school. Steve's hobby was playing war games. In his war games, he recreated famous battles. Two people could play, so Steve invited Ken over to play war games on Saturday afternoons and evenings.

When they took breaks from the game to eat homemade pizza, Joan tried talking to Ken. He was unresponsive at first. This continued all winter. However, within six weeks,

I had lost my side of our bed because Ken was sitting there talking to Joan for increasing periods of time. Ken's attitude toward his other family members changed, and his grades headed back toward straight *A*'s. Joan's love, insight, and advice changed Ken and his attitudes.

OCTOBER 11, 1980: 9:20 P.M.

> Help those who cannot see (like doubting Thomas). Although they are not blind, they cannot see. Help those who hear but do not listen—who do not really hear. By decreasing yourself, I (God) increase you. The time is getting shorter, but scaring people is not the answer. We think of Jesus as a King, but we are all kings if we want to be. There is nothing wrong with being on a pedestal if we are willing to share the pedestal with many others. Give people (like doubting Thomas) a little of what they want to hear and then slip in the message. Jesus, you are love, not lust, and only capable of loving from the heart. Bill and I are so close; when one hurts, the other feels it. Every word out of our mouths should be to glorify you, not to disgrace you. In Jesus name, we thank you.

OCTOBER 12, 1980: 7:50 P.M.

Teach people to love themselves. From childhood, we learn to be humble. But Jesus was humble, the image of God, a teacher, a prophet, loved the little children, and the Messiah. It became so hard on Him when people judged Him wrong. He would say, "Oh thou high and mighty . . ." People from my hometown don't believe me. You have eyes but don't see; ears but don't hear. It is time to wake up. Never let your pride make you ashamed of your Holy Father in any way. I, Jesus Christ, get so frustrated, I get hurt. I love. I need love.

In spite of Joanie's boundless love and smiles that lit up our room, I was still preoccupied with work at times. I had made the self-centered statement, "I am a self-made man!" Then on August 29, 1980, at 3 a.m., the Lord woke me. In an angry, deep voice, he said, "Do you not cast the first stone? The children need her, but you don't need anyone. I have given you everything but you still don't believe. Hell is for eternity!!"

That scared Satan out of me. I changed that night, and became a born-again Christian. I realized that I am a God-made man. Joan slept through my experience.

SEPTEMBER 25, 1980: 11:20 P.M.

He had to break you (Bill) before He could make you.

SEPTEMBER 27, 1980: 9:35 A.M

My William, my son, was lost and now found. No numbness and dullness again.

The Lord speaks to very few. Why me? Because I was in love with and married to His special Little One. I highly value His loving gift to me. I help her any way I can help her.

CHAPTER 8

KIDNEY INFECTIONS

J oan started having severe kidney infections in 1979. Her kidney pain was severe. Her kidneys were barely functioning. Medication helped sometimes, but on many days, Joanie wound up on her back in pain.

SEPTEMBER 27, 1980: 9:35 A.M.

We are a mirror for the world to see how Jesus lived. In my illness, I have gained all eternity for the things I have had to bear. Satan causes bad things to happen many times; not necessarily Satan acting in me but in someone else who affects me. I am never going to give up for Jesus. In going through all these adversities, Jesus said, "You lose precious things but you gain eternity. Man complicates things that God wants to be easy."

The severe kidney infections continued throughout 1980 and 1981. When Joan got discouraged, I would read to her our favorite scripture from *The Living Bible*, Romans 8:31–39. I would insert Joan's name into the passage to encourage her:

> What can we ever say to such wonderful things as these? If God is on (Joan's) side, who can ever be against (her)? 8:32: Since he did not spare even his own son for (Joan) but gave him up for all, won't he also surely give (Joan) everything else? 8:33: Who dares accuse (Joan) whom God has chosen for his own? Will God? No! He is the one who has forgiven (Joan) and given (her) right standing with himself. 8:34: Who then will condemn (Joan)? Will Christ? No! For he is the one who died for (Joan) and came back to life again for (her) and is sitting at the place of highest honor next to God, pleading for (her) there in Heaven. 8:35: Who then can ever keep Christ's love from (Joan)? When (Joan) has trouble or calamity, when (she) is hunted down or destroyed, is it because He doesn't love (her) anymore? And if (Joan) is hungry, or penniless, or in danger, or threatened with death, has God deserted (her)? 8:36: No, for the Scriptures tell us that for his sake, (Joan) must be ready to face death at every moment of the day—(Joan) is like sheep awaiting slaughter; 8:37: but despite all this, overwhelming victory is (hers) through Christ who loved (her) enough to die for (her). 8:38: For I am convinced that nothing can ever separate (Joan) from his love. Death can't, and life

can't. The angels won't, and all the powers of hell itself cannot keep God's love away. (Joan's) fears for today, (her) worries about tomorrow, 8:39 or where (she) is—high above the sky, or in the deepest ocean—nothing will ever be able to separate (Joan) from the love of God demonstrated by our Lord Jesus Christ when he died for (her)."

We knew that Reverend Oral Roberts had built a ten-story medical center a couple of years earlier on his university campus. We made an appointment at the center for Joan to have a complete kidney examination. On Thanksgiving 1981, we drove the station wagon, with Joan lying down in the back, from Indiana to Oklahoma for the appointment.

After a day and a half of examinations, the female head of the Urology Department sat down with Joan. With tears in her eyes, she told Joan that the kidney infection had badly scarred her kidneys. They were smaller than normal and only functioning at twenty percent of their capacity. Joan would die in six months from kidney failure. Nothing could be done to help her.

Oh yes, there was something to help Joan! Prayers and the Lord's healing. We had prayed many times before that day for the Lord to heal her kidneys. We prayed even more fervently for Joanie's healing. The Lord answered this time! Joanie never had another kidney infection. The twenty percent of her kidneys worked fine for the next twenty-eight and a half years. The Lord still had more for her to do here; including changing more lives.

This was Joanie's third healing miracle by the Lord:

1. The full-bottle overdose of sleeping pills.

2. The healing from the myasthenia gravis.

3. The healing of Joan's kidneys, including the end of the kidney infections.

OCTOBER 12, 1980: 7:55 P.M.

> I died on the cross. Thirsty. Miracles do not have to happen but for only a very few they do happen. Oh, how I hurt. If I do not cry out, they will not think I am human. The end is near. All of ye who nailed me to the cross, physical pain is not like mental pain. Mental pain is much worse. I leave you. Father, take me.

"Yea though I walk through the valley of the shadow of death, I will fear no evil." (Psalm 23:4)

CHAPTER 9

TRAUMATIC EVENTS

I n early February 1978, Joan went downstairs to boil water to make tea. She turned on the stove under a pan of cooking oil she had used the night before to make french fries. Then she went back upstairs. Our four children had already left for school. I was in Washington, D.C., at a national conference.

Joan came downstairs ten to fifteen minutes later and saw the overheated cooking oil had exploded into flames and started a raging fire in our kitchen's plastic false ceiling. She ran next door barefooted, in the snow, to call the fire department. The fire department arrived soon and put out the fire.

All of the carpet downstairs and on the two stairways was ruined from the water. The kitchen damage was severe. The downstairs furniture, curtains, clothes, and walls were all severely water- and smoke-damaged. Our homeowner's insurance company hired a company to do all of the repairs. This was the biggest job the repair company had ever done. The first night, we slept elsewhere. The second night, we were back in our four upstairs bedrooms. That night at 11:00 p.m. Joan received a phone call from a man with a deep, slurred voice who said, "Burn, Baby, Burn!"

The home repairs required fifteen weeks to complete. I went to work every day. Our four children went to school every day. Joan was alone with the repair people and very unhappy with their work. They broke pieces of our best china dining set, antique porcelain, and glass-ware. Clothing and curtains were taken and not returned. Items were stolen. Joan cleaned up their messes, became increasingly upset, and lost over fifteen pounds.

Joan was also pregnant. Because of all of her work, stress, and anguish from the fire, she lay down on our bathroom floor and miscarried our five-month-old fetus son four months after the fire. She was alone in our home.

We employed a lawyer to sue our insurance company and the repair company for their mishandling of the repairs from the fire. Joan wrote a letter to our lawyer fourteen months after the fire, explaining some of her stress and strain and the loss of our baby son. Our whole family was affected, but the greatest burden of this trau-matic event was on the Lord's Little One, Joanie. That burden continued for many months after the fire. Was Satan complicating this mess every chance he could get?

Then Joan started having grand mal seizures in October 1983.

OCTOBER 2, 1984

The nurses and doctors told my family the worst was ahead. In less than twenty-four hours, my small body had at least four wicked seizures. These seizures were so violent that I had to be tied down, padding everywhere. They put me in intensive care. There was very little hope for me. I was in critical condition for three or four days. The doctors were afraid of brain damage.

Our Heavenly Father really saved my life in many ways. After the immediate danger was over, I was in a regular room for another ten days. Each day was a little better.

The seizures stopped and never occurred again. The reason for the starting and stopping of the seizures was never diagnosed, but we know that the Lord healed his Little One once again.

CHAPTER 10

JOAN'S WISDOM

JANUARY 17, 1981: 12:30 A.M.

Joan is not the head of the family, but is the spiritual leader and backbone of her family. One day, she will be remembered and honored when she is gone. She is the healer through Jesus and specially chosen.

I (Joan) can see Him and talk to Him. I know suffering and must not suffer anymore. Be joyous unto the Lord, for we have an insight. Without this insight, there would be no hope. I am not of this earth. It would be so much simpler to be human. Bill, no more guilt trips for Joan (for weakness), or they will count against you.

SEPTEMBER 27, 1980: 9:50 A.M.

We are able to take things selfishly but somehow rationalize it away. When the whole universe and eternity is given to you, we are suspicious of God and resist. We complicate life when life must stay simple in the Lord. We take wages from work, because we earned them. But the Lord gives freely and we are suspicious. What's the catch? We know that we are doing right by the blessings that we receive inside and outside. We have inner peace and we do not fear the future.

AUGUST 30, 1980

I feel gifted, because I have seen life through many eyes: sickness, poverty, happiness, love, guilt, alcoholism, and an understanding that most people can't believe. Speak through us to glorify your name. Give us a chance to convert or help in your name. Let my own life story be heard by millions, for their need to know of salvation in Jesus' name. Give Bill and me a oneness known only to you. Put bitterness and jealousy in Satan's hands where they belong. Let us minister together and let our love grow through you, in Jesus' Name.

Between 1982 and 1986, our four children were married. We now have thirteen grandchildren. Through the years, Joan and I have loved and enjoyed our grandchildren. Joan remained weak and did not have much stamina, but her boundless love, care, sparkling eyes, and a smile that lit up a room surrounded us all.

Joan and I went on vacation in early January 1991 to Sanibel Island. For ten days, we enjoyed perfect, eighty-two-degree weather each day. Joan did great and lay in the sun each day. Then we flew from Fort Myers, Florida, to the Indianapolis airport. We deplaned in minus-twenty-degree weather. Joan got cold and caught a cold. When Joan was still sick two weeks later, she said, "I can't survive another cold Indiana winter." That is when the Lord took over our lives and started opening doors.

I had thirty-one years of service with General Motors. I asked for my retirement printout. My regular retirement would not give us enough to live on. Joanie and I prayed that somehow the Lord would open the doors so I could retire. Then we learned that General Motors was offering a "special early retirement" package to reduce the salaried head count by seven percent. The package would go into effect on September 1, 1991.

The workload for my New Products group had been decreasing. I talked to our chief engineer and proposed that my ten engineers be moved under two existing supervisors. My job would be eliminated with a reduction of one salaried head count.

Our chief engineer put me on the "special early retirement" list. That let us receive an additional $1,400 per month retirement pay until I drew Social Security at age sixty-two. We would then receive enough per month that we could cover all of our bills and expenses. I retired on September 1, 1991. All the other employees, except three, on the "special early retirement" list were age fifty-seven or older. Two of the three had poor health. I was fifty-three and in excellent health, but my wife's health was not good.

We drove to Fort Myers, Florida, in mid-October 1991, rented a furnished house, and enjoyed a warm fall and winter. Joanie's health was good all winter. We drove back to our home in Indiana in late April 1992. We happily visited with our children and grandchildren that summer.

OCTOBER 11, 1980: 10:30 P.M.

> For as the Little One says, strangers are friends we haven't met.

Joan was kind and loving to everyone she met, though her weakness would stop her at times.

If an earthly king ruled all of the kingdoms, he would never have enough wealth to buy wisdom.

SEPTEMBER 25, 1980: 11:25 P.M.

> Praise brings anointing. Anointing brings peace that passes all understanding. I (Joan) am an anointed minister by Jesus. The Word is—is of Jesus. I know that knowledge is given from the Lord. Don't let life disappoint you or it will pass you by. It is a gift. Put God first and every problem in the world will be solved.

OCTOBER 11, 1980: 10:40 P.M.

> Don't pick the Bible apart.

James L. Johnson quote, "God doesn't mind our humanity when we are frightened." But if we ask him, He will protect us and guide us in the right way.

Oral Roberts said to Joan on the phone, "He who is in you is greater than he who is in the world." (1 John 4:4)

OCTOBER 11, 1980: 6:15 P.M.

Your education is Heavenly and not of the world. If you call yourself stupid, you are talking about mine.

OCTOBER 11, 1980: 6:20 P.M.

I am a selfish God. I made you. I love you. All I want is for you to love me.

OCTOBER 11, 1980: 6:25 P.M.

God wants us to know about Him. That is why He sent Jesus to tell us about His Father.

OCTOBER 3, 1980: 5:55 A.M.

Wisdom comes slowly. A little wisdom will be given to you. If you are grateful in a little wisdom, you will be given much more. This wisdom is not learned but Heaven sent.

The Little One

September 25, 1980: 10:45 P.M.

> Don't be impatient! Take time. My Little One is so
> excited! Talk to her. Don't let a word escape. So much
> is to be written. This tiny one was sent to carry on,
> to make peace in this world. She has such limited
> strength. She relies on me for her strength each day.
> She is well in her mind. Her memory must be very
> sharp. You must never forget. In listening you learn.

In October 1992, we drove to Fort Myers and leased a
different house than in the previous winter. The house had
three bedrooms, a swimming pool nearby, and was ten
to fifteen minutes by car from the great beaches at Fort
Myers and Sanibel Island. Each of our four children and
their families were welcome and stayed with us while on
their vacations. Joan's health was good. We returned to
Indiana for the summer of 1993 and leased the same house
for the coming winter.

After returning to Fort Myers in November 1993, we
received word that our grandsons, Michael, age four,
and David, age two, had been taken from their mother in
Lansing, Michigan, and placed in foster care. This was the
third time in their short lives they had been placed in foster
care. Our youngest son, Michael Alan, was their father but
was separated from their mother.

We prayed and felt strongly that their mother would never get them back. If left in foster care, they could be adopted away from our family forever. We had to do everything possible to obtain custody of Michael and David.

CHAPTER 11

JOAN'S LOVE

I told Joan that if we were able to get Michael and David, she would be their wonderful, wise, loving, and caring mother. I would take care of everything else such as cooking the meals, doing laundry, playing with them, and taking them to doctor appointments, school, school functions, activities, and church. My health and strength continued to be excellent.

We contacted Paul, the Social Services person responsible for Michael and David. Paul recommended that we write a letter to the Lansing judge, outlining our relationship and qualifications, to obtain permanent custody of our two grandsons. We wrote a several-page letter in late January 1994, stating the requested information. We sent a copy to Paul.

Paul informed us in late February that the first custody hearing before the judge would be held on March 3, 1994. I flew from Fort Myers to Lansing to be at the hearing. I learned nothing at the hearing. I talked to Paul and visited Pat and Joe, who were excellent foster parents, and had fun with Michael and David. Michael was very angry over how he had been taken away from his mother. He roamed the house at night and Pat tied him to his bed with strips of sheet. He also would take his anger out on young, innocent David.

Pat took Michael and David to Sarasota in April—to see Pat's mother—and contacted us. We invited them to our house in Ft. Myers for a great day. We then invited Pat, Michael, and David to go with us to the Magic Kingdom. We had a great time, again. I still remember the elevated basket ride on a taut wire, transporting us at sunset.

We were back in Indiana in late May and attended the next meeting before the judge in early June. Again, we felt no progress was made. We talked to Paul and he assured us he was working for us. Since we did not have progress after two important meetings, I felt he was not helping, and maybe he was working against us. We talked to Pat for half an hour and stated our doubts that Paul was helping us. "Should we get a lawyer?" we asked.

Pat said, "Yes."

"Can you recommend one?"

She gave us the name of Phil, a lawyer who had specialized in custody and adoption cases for over twenty years. Phil was working for us by mid-June . . . and he got the boys for us. We attended the court hearing on September 1. Not much happened except Lawyer Phil obtained a temporary release for Michael and David to come back to

Anderson with us. We had to return with them to Lansing for a September 8th hearing, set up by Phil, for us to obtain permanent custody of Michael and David.

The boys' mother attended that hearing, only the second of the four hearings she attended. She had missed the previous two meetings because she had slit her wrists early in the morning and was in the hospital. As a nurse's aid, she knew how deeply to slit her wrists for the wound to be fatal. This was her self-administered excuse to miss court.

But, she did not want Joan and me to get our grandsons, so she appeared at this court hearing. However, she clearly did not want them anymore. Her first argument was that Joan was not strong or well enough to take care of the two very active boys. Our reply was that I had retired from General Motors in 1991. Caring for and raising the boys would be a full-time job for both Joan and me. My health was perfect and I was very active. That argument was cancelled.

Her second argument was that we were Christian fanatics. We had stated that we would raise Michael and David as Christians. They would be in church every Sunday. Lawyer Phil obtained an agreement for us to go through psychological testing to determine if we were fit to raise two young children.

So, we returned two weeks later for psychological testing. Joanie and I separately went through written and oral exams for one and a half days. Our evaluation results showed we were normal and would make good parents. Of course, we had the proof of having already raising our own children successfully.

We took Michael and David to Fort Myers in the middle of October. Joanie, the boys, and I flew to Lansing, Michigan, for our final court hearing before the judge on November 3, 1994. We were then named Michael and David's permanent guardians.

The flight was Michael and David's first plane ride. They were fascinated by the planes and the loading process. When we took off, their eyes were as big as saucers! Michael was so excited. "We're off the ground! Boy, I like this! Cars look like ants moving around!" he exclaimed.

Joan and I have always said that one of the joys of being a parent is watching and sharing in your child's excitement and wonder in seeing and experiencing new things. We relive events through their eyes and reactions. The experiences were kind of like a "second" childhood for Joan and me.

Over the next months, we had several precious moments. Just three weeks later, Michael told Joan, "Grandma, you need to get your hair done." When Joan came out of the beauty shop, Michael said to her, "You look beauuuuuutiful!"

David said, "What a babe!!"

On Christmas Day, Michael had a serious discussion with Joan. He explained that the Santa in the picture with him and David was not the real one because "he had wires holding his whiskers." Joan calmly explained that he was one of Santa's helpers. We watched *Ernest Saves Christmas* on Christmas night. After watching the final scene in which Santa hires Ernest to be his driver, Joan pointed out that he was, "another Santa's helper." Later, Michael asked how Santa got a new bike into his backpack and onto his sleigh.

Another time, David was playing in the living room. He came up to Joan three different times and asked if she had time for a hug.

"Of course! I always have time for a hug," she replied.

Once, I gave the boys Beer Nuts. David went running in to see Grandma and said, "Grandpa gave us these nuts. They are really good! Do you want one?" He took one of the nuts out of his mouth and offered it to Grandma.

Joanie would say to the boys two or three times a day, "I love you." They would say back, "I love you, Grandma." Lots of hugs and kisses were exchanged.

David said some of the cutest things. One night, Joan was rubbing his back in bed to make him sleepy. He said, "And I'll not move a muscle (because he was kind of squirmy) and I'll zip my lips (he talked a lot) and I won't fiddle-fart around! (he fooled around and passed gas a lot)."

Michael and David were truly a blessing to us from the Lord. We thoroughly enjoyed raising them. They kept us "young at heart." We raised Michael and David as Christians and to love and rely on the Lord, just as we did. We raised them with Christian morality and principles so they would know what is right and wrong in their thoughts and actions. We even changed churches to obtain a better church school, youth programs, and youth leadership for the boys.

Michael and David gave us purpose in our retirement. In looking back, the Lord healed Joanie in 1981 from kidney infections and extended her life twenty-eight and one half years so she could be Michael and David's loving, hugging, wise, and smiling mother.

The Lord still wasn't finished changing our family's life. I kept a journal of all of the cute, funny things Michael and David did the first four or five years. I wrote a letter to their father in Indiana every week, filled with the cute things Michael and David did. Soon after we got the boys, their father hit rock bottom and gave his life to the Lord. He was a changed person. I wanted him to sell his Indiana business and move down to live with us so he could enjoy the boys and help raise them.

In 2000, Michael Alan finally sold his antique furniture business and box truck. He moved to Fort Myers to live with us and his sons. They are great together.

I told Michael Alan that he could not make a living in Florida refinishing and selling antique furniture. Florida residents bought new furniture painted white with glass inserts and chromed pieces. Since he was an excellent furniture salesperson, I suggested he sell new furniture. He received three job offers and took a job with Havertys Furniture Company. With the busiest furniture sales time of the year just beginning, he did very well in sales.

As part of the Lord's plan, a woman named Jackie also started working at Havertys' soon afterward. Jackie and Michael Alan started dating. They fell in love and were married a year later. To be close to their sons, they bought a house two blocks from where we lived. Their love lasts forever!

CHAPTER 12

50TH ANNIVERSARY

Joan continued to be weak, but she always had a heart full of love for all of us. Her smile and beautiful brown eyes always lit up the room. However, her legs would not consistently support her body weight after 2004. She fell many times trying to walk. Was Satan pushing her down? The Lord continued to protect her, even in her falls. She never broke a bone.

In 2007, we took Joan to the best myasthenia gravis doctor in the Fort Myers area. Could the myasthenia gravis be back and causing the weakness? The doctor put Joanie through extensive tests and determined the myasthenia gravis was not back. An MRI (magnetic resonance imaging) with contrast was run on her brain and everything was normal. At the cancer center, a doctor ran extensive blood tests. He found no cancer or abnormalities. Neither doctor could explain her weakness.

On August 25, 2007, Joanie and I celebrated our 50th wedding anniversary with our six strong, healthy, successful, and loved children. Thank you, Lord, for blessing my life with Joanie, the love of my life. Thank you, Lord, for blessing Joan and me with six strong, healthy children to raise, love, enjoy, and teach about you.

SEPTEMBER 25, 1980: 11:00 P.M.

> Just because you are sick, God loves you. He isn't mad at you. Gold goes through several processes to refine it. The same is for you. Your trials are refining you. Oh, how He loves you and me. Yes. We are so impatient and He is so patient with us.

OCTOBER 11, 1980: 11:15 P.M.

> You are blessed, my son! Always listen. Her breath gets short. One day you will have to do all of the talking. Get it all on paper. Some things are only known between her and me. Barrels couldn't hold all of her knowledge and life. It is I, Jesus, that is in the Little One. Good night. Peace be with you. Say it . . . Jesus, Jesus, Jesus! Where? In Heaven. Where? In me. Jesus is in me.

Through sickness and health, God brought us through. All of Satan's dirty tricks tried to destroy, but have not succeeded.

CHAPTER 13

SATAN'S ATTACKS

The year 2009 was very difficult for Joan due to bungled surgeries and lots of pain. In early March, we scheduled an eye exam for Joan with Dr. Quick. We simply wanted a prescription for new glasses. Her previous exam had been over ten years earlier. At the doctor's office, we received a high-pressure pitch on how to get *guaranteed perfect vision* so Joan would no longer need glasses. They insisted they were experts at performing an expensive surgery which would involve inserting a new prescription lens into each eye. The surgery on Joan's left eye was done in mid-March and the surgery on the right eye was completed in mid-April. We administered eye drops every three or four hours and she experienced on and off eye pain. By August 1, Joan was blind in the right eye and her vision in the left eye was worse than before the surgery. At an eye exam on August 10, she passed out in the examining chair. With our lawyer, we filed charges against Dr. Quick for false promises. We also filed a complaint with the Florida Department of Health. We wished we had only gotten a prescription for new glasses.

In early July, Joan had a bad toothache. After two appointments over two weeks with Dr. Ace, he verified the tooth could not be saved. So we took her to have the tooth, a back molar, pulled. After the tooth was pulled, Dr. Ace gave Joan pain pills to take for seven days. She had to be on a liquid diet for those seven days. Instead of the pain going away in seven days, it took thirty days. But, the pain pills ran out after fourteen days. She also stayed on the liquid diet for thirty days and lost fifteen pounds.

Prior to having her tooth pulled, I helped Joan walk around our large house four to six times a day. But she never walked again after the tooth was pulled. Satan was out to get Joan!

On September 1, Joan started doing two strange things. First, she was asking if her mother was still at our house even though her mother had died twenty-five years earlier. Second, she asked when were we going back home (to Anderson, Indiana). We had sold that house back in 1998 and had bought our present, only home in Fort Myers that same year. I talked to our family doctor about this in late September. He didn't know what to do.

On Sunday, October 4, Joan had a seizure. She stared straight ahead without seeing. She could not hear and she could not speak. This continued into Monday, October 5. An ambulance picked her up at 9 a.m. and took her to the hospital. I next saw her in her hospital room at 10:30 a.m. She spoke to me and was normal. Was this the Lord's way of getting her to the hospital for testing?

The next day, an MRI revealed white spots in her brain; one was an inch in diameter and three or four others were each one-quarter inch in diameter. On October 6, the surgeon took tissue from the one-inch location and found it was malignant.

Chemotherapy was the only way to eliminate the white cancer spots from the brain. But the doctor was also afraid the chemotherapy would completely stop the twenty percent activity of Joan's kidneys. The doctor first administered one-eighth of the full dosage of chemotherapy. The treatment had no affect on her kidneys. The second chemotherapy treatment was one-fourth of the full dosage. Still no affect on the kidneys. We had prayed to our Lord God Almighty that Joanie would be healed by making the chemotherapy stronger. I asked for another MRI with contrast and the hospital ran it. The white malignant spots were so small that they couldn't be measured. I asked our chemotherapy doctor, "Isn't that remarkable healing for that low of a chemotherapy dosage?"

He replied, "That is remarkable, but no miracle!" He didn't believe in our healing Lord.

The third chemotherapy was one-fourth full dosage and was given over Thanksgiving with no affect on the kidneys. But our primary oncologist did not check on Joan at all during this hospital stay. His colleagues checked on her daily. This session was bungled badly and required a stay of nine days. The previous treatment under our primary oncologist only took three and one-half days. I requested an MRI with contrast. They ran an MRI without contrast (in which the image was all brown). It could not be compared to the "with contrast" image.

Joan and I met with the oncologist on December 17. We agreed that Joan needed an MRI with contrast to see if the cancer was gone. Joan had to get over her cold and have good blood test results before the oncologist would authorize an outpatient MRI with contrast for Joan.

On December 28 and 29, I was thrilled to see the old Joanie again. She was talking, smiling, and watching her favorite TV shows. On December 30, the physical therapist, who had been recommended by the oncologist, came. He sat Joan in the wheelchair for a half hour and exercised her legs. Then we laid her back in bed. Her body was trembling all over. She was the weakest I have ever seen her. She had no strength left to fight cancer.

The next day, she had completely changed. She could only answer simple questions with "yes" or "no." She could no longer concentrate on any television shows. Moving her arms or her body was very painful.

Through more bungling, the blood sample did not get pulled until January 15. The test results were all fine and the MRI with contrast was completed in the afternoon of

January 27. The oncologist reviewed the results late on January 29. He called me to say that the cancer was much worse and nothing further could be done. I was shocked! I thought the Lord would complete her healing and the cancer would be gone.

Thinking back, her condition changed drastically on December 30. She didn't have any strength or resistance and the cancer took over and spread. She also developed a stomach ulcer from the chemotherapy drugs in early January which added to her pain when she ate.

Hope Hospice took over Joan's care at home on February 1. They gave her strong pain medication on February 2 in the afternoon. She fell asleep and never woke up. I can still see her final mouth movements saying, without sound, "I love you" before she was sleeping.

SEPTEMBER 27, 1980: 9:35 A.M.

> In my illness, I have gained all eternity for things that I have had to bear. Satan causes bad things to happen many times, not necessarily Satan in me but as Satan in someone else that affects me [such as Dr. Quick, Dr. Ace, and the oncologist]. I am never going to give up for Jesus.

CHAPTER 14

HEAVENLY PEACE

J oan was given twenty-eight more years to live in 1981. The Lord healed her of the severe kidney infections that the doctor said would take her life in six months. Joanie would be our grandsons' (Michael and David) wonderful, wise, loving, and caring mother starting in 1994. I was also blessed with the extra years with a wise, loving, and caring wife. Joan did a great job with the Lord's guidance. Michael and David never doubted their grandmother and grandfather's love. And Joan had completed her job: Michael was twenty and David was nineteen years old. Both were high school graduates and almost ready for the world.

On February 6, 2010, my best friend in Heaven, Jesus, took my best friend on earth, Joanie, to Heaven to be with Him. No more pain, weakness, or discomfort. Simply heavenly peace. We believe that her best-friend dog, Midgie, is with Joanie in Heaven.

I continue to remember Joanie's words of wisdom:

OCTOBER 11, 1980: 6:10 P.M.

The streets of Heaven are paved with gold. Do you know why gold? Gold is pure, refined, beautiful—fired and purified—the ultimate—in Heaven. Did I say that?

SEPTEMBER 27, 1980: 9:35 A.M.

We complicate life when life must stay simple in the Lord. We take wages from work because we earned them. But the Lord gives freely, and we are suspicious. What's the catch? We know that we are doing right by the blessings that we receive; inside and outside. Inner peace—and we do not fear the future.

To enter my Father's world is a gift for all who receive Him. One only has to put God above all else and know to give your life to Him. Not only joy will come through earthly life, but death will never frighten you. Entering Heaven is but an exciting extension of life. It is normal to have fear of the unknown. But learning of "the light" only makes you positive of God's promise of eternal life.

Upon entering, Heaven is not to be feared, but only a gift from the one who gave you life. Praise the Lord.

OCTOBER 7, 1980: 6:20 P.M.

> When something is taken away [Joanie], the Lord
> will give us even more in return, because He loves us.

I am looking forward to the Lord's next gift. But this gift will be very hard to top: the wonderful blessing, love of my life, mother of our six children, and my wife, Joanie.

EPILOGUE

You have read how the Holy Spirit and love that was placed in Joan Webel Johnson's heart at birth meant that she was a special child of the Lord. She had a special life and special work for the Lord. Although Satan tried to interfere with illness, the much stronger Lord healed Joan and led her through many wonderful events in her life.

Why Joanie? Joanie proves that the smallest (the Little One), the last to get theirs, the weakest, the poorest, the mediator, the insecure, those who don't complain, and can always smile, win out over Satan's evil intents. They continue to pray and believe in Jesus, His love, and saving powers. They never give up fighting Satan's challenges. They know Jesus will get them through to success.

SEPTEMBER 25, 1980

> To prove that the mightiest and bravest soldiers can be so small, no background, poverty, sickness—my Little One came out of all of it with no bitterness.

Her education is heavenly—<u>she is chosen</u>.

While we lived in Martinsville, Indiana, I remember Joanie smiled all the time. She was easy to talk to and she laughed, had lots of friends, had love in her heart and cared for everyone. Our match was made in Heaven. Through her love, she helped me become a born-again Christian with Jesus as my best friend in Heaven.

Every one of us can have this same Holy Spirit and love in our hearts by opening our hearts and inviting Jesus to fill us with His love. You will then care for, love, and serve others, just as Joanie did. Only the love that comes from Jesus can give you true joy and happiness in your life.

The Scriptures say, "His love for us endures forever." The Lord, in anger, said to me, "The children need her, but you don't need anyone. Hell is for eternity." The Lord loved me through forty-two years of church going, kept me healthy, and gave me Joan. I changed that night and became a born-again Christian. I have talked (prayed) to my best friend in heaven, Jesus, every morning since. I pray you will also find the true love and peace from God that helped us have true joy through all of the hardships we faced.

Open your hearts and receive Jesus and the Holy Spirit and love for everyone—like Joanie. Change your life!!! If you need help in making this change, call Bill Johnson at 239-489-3941, in Fort Myers, Florida.

IF YOU'RE A FAN OF THIS BOOK, PLEASE TELL OTHERS...

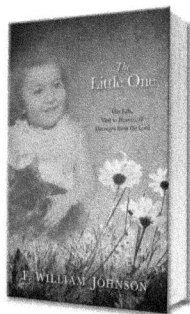

- Write about *The Little One* on your blog, Twitter, MySpace, and Facebook page.
- Suggest *The Little One* to friends.
- When you're in a bookstore, ask them if they carry the book. The book is available through all major distributors, so any bookstore that does not have *The Little One* in stock can easily order it.
- Write a positive review of *The Little One* on www.amazon.com.
- Send my publisher, HigherLife Publishing, suggestions on websites, conferences, and events you know of where this book could be offered at media@ahigherlife.com.
- Purchase additional copies to give away as gifts.

CONNECT WITH ME...

To learn more about *The Little One*, please contact the author at 239-489-3941.You may also contact my publisher directly:

> HigherLife Publishing
> 400 Fontana Circle
> Building 1 – Suite 105
> Oviedo, Florida 32765
> Phone: (407) 563-4806
> Email: media@ahigherlife.com

Coming Soon...

The

Little One

∽

Raising Two Grandsons

by
GRANDMA JOAN JOHNSON
and
GRANDPA F. WILLIAM JOHNSON

This is the next book in the series, showing the joy of grandparents raising grandchildren.